W9-DHX-480

Model T to Self-Driving Cars
Then to Now Tech

By Jennifer Colby

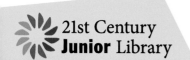
21st Century
Junior Library

CHERRY LAKE Publishing

Published in the United States of America by
Cherry Lake Publishing
Ann Arbor, Michigan
www.cherrylakepublishing.com

Content Adviser: Adam Fulton Johnson, PhD History of Science and Technology, University of Michigan
Reading Adviser: Marla Conn, MS, Ed., Literacy specialist, Read-Ability, Inc.

Photo Credits: ©RUBEN M RAMOS/Shutterstock.com, Cover, 1 [left]; ©metamorworks/Shutterstock.com, Cover, 2 [right]; Library of Congress, LC-USZ62-118659, 4; ©Mary Evans PictureLibrary Ltd/agefotostock.com, 6, 16; Library of Congress, LC-USZ62-118671, 8; ©VintageCorner/alamy.com, 10; ©gregobagel/iStock.com, 12; ©Bobby Watkins/Shutterstock.com, 14; ©Olga Marc/Shutterstock.com, 18; ©Zapp2Photo/Shutterstock.com, 20

Copyright © 2020 by Cherry Lake Publishing
All rights reserved. No part of this book may be reproduced or utilized in any
form or by any means without written permission from the publisher.

Library of Congress Cataloging-in-Publication Data
Names: Colby, Jennifer, 1971- author.
Title: Model T to self-driving cars : then to now tech / Jennifer Colby.
Description: Ann Arbor : Cherry Lake Publishing, [2019] | Series: Then to now tech |
    Includes bibliographical references and index. | Audience: K to
    grade 3.
Identifiers: LCCN 2019004224| ISBN 9781534147294 (hardcover) | ISBN
    9781534150157 (pbk.) | ISBN 9781534148727 (pdf) | ISBN 9781534151581
    (hosted ebook)
Subjects: LCSH: Automobiles—History—Juvenile literature. |
    Automobiles—Technological innovations—Juvenile literature.
Classification: LCC TL15 .C635 2019 | DDC 629.22209—dc23
LC record available at https://lccn.loc.gov/2019004224

Cherry Lake Publishing would like to acknowledge the work of the Partnership for 21st Century Skills.
Please visit www.p21.org for more information.

Printed in the United States of America
Corporate Graphics

CONTENTS

5 **Tin Lizzie**

7 **Early Cars**

11 **Postwar Boom**

19 **Designed for the Future**

22 Glossary

23 Find Out More

24 Index

24 About the Author

4 CYL. MODEL T
FORD, 1908

© The GROGAN PHOTO COMPANY Danville, Ill.

The Ford Model T was nicknamed the Tin Lizzie.

Tin Lizzie

Do you know someone who owns a car? Maybe your family does. Just over 100 years ago, car ownership was only for the very rich. When Henry Ford started **production** on the Model T in 1908, cars became more affordable for everyone.

Ford invented the assembly line for his Model T and changed
the way goods were made.

Early Cars

Generally, the public did not like cars. They needed constant **maintenance**. And they were expensive. But the Model T changed people's opinions of cars. It was **durable** and cheap. Over 15 million Model Ts were built from 1908 to 1927. It was the first car to be built on an **assembly line**.

8 CYL. CORD, 1937
© The GROGAN PHOTO COMPANY Danville, Ill.

This Cord Automobile was considered a luxury vehicle in 1937.

In the early 1900s, cars were being built around the world. As technology advanced, car **manufacturers** began building cars with new safety and **performance** features. New **convenience** items were also added, including radios and heaters.

Think!

The 1908 Ford Model T sold for $850. It sold for less than $300 in 1925! Why do you think that is?

New cars were built after World War II.

Postwar Boom

Car manufacturing was shut down during World War II. Car factories built weapons of war instead. All resources were focused on the war effort. Everyone had to keep their old cars running. But after the war, the demand for new cars was huge! With raw materials available again and soldiers coming home, car sales soared.

An early Volkswagen Beetle was also called the "People's Car."

New designs made cars more attractive and useful. They also became more powerful and could drive at faster speeds.

In Germany, a new car was designed to provide cheap transportation. It proved to be very popular. The Volkswagen Beetle is the longest-running and most-manufactured car ever designed!

In the 1950s, U.S. President Dwight D. Eisenhower proposed a system of roads that would connect the country from east to west and north to south.

With all these new cars, people needed somewhere to drive them. The old system of roads had been designed for horses and wagons. It needed an **upgrade**. In the United States and Europe, new systems of **highways** began to be planned. Soon travel became faster and simpler.

Make a Guess!

The Federal-Aid Highway Act of 1956 authorized 41,000 miles (66,000 kilometers) of interstate highways. How many miles of highway do you think were actually built? Ask an adult to help you search the internet to find out.

Sometimes lines for gas were so long, people had to direct traffic.

Most cars of the time were **fueled** by gasoline. Gasoline is made from oil. Oil is a natural resource that comes out of the ground. Most of the oil used around the world is found in the Middle East. In the 1970s, gas prices rose sky high! It got people thinking about the future.

Look!

In the early 1970s, gasoline cost around 36 cents a gallon. But by the end of the decade, it cost 86 cents a gallon. In today's dollars, that would be $2.81 per gallon. How much is gasoline per gallon today? Look at the price sign at a local gas station.

Electric cars run on electricity.

Designed for the Future

Today, innovations in technology allow car makers to explore other options. The idea of electric cars is very popular. They help reduce air pollution by using a cleaner fuel. Self-driving technology is being developed. These cars can drive by themselves!

Driverless cars will become very common in the future.

In the next 20 years, self-driving cars will dominate the road! New road systems will have to be built to **accommodate** cars without drivers. The goal is to make driving more **efficient** and safer for everyone.

Ask Questions!

Would you ride in a self-driving car? Take a poll. Ask your friends and family how they feel.

GLOSSARY

accommodate (uh-KAH-muh-date) to provide what is needed or wanted

assembly line (uh-SEM-blee LINE) a line of machines, equipment, and workers in a factory that builds a product by passing work from one station to the next until the product is finished

convenience (kuhn-VEEN-yuhns) something that makes you more comfortable or allows you to do things more easily

durable (DOOR-uh-buhl) staying strong and in good condition over a long period of time

efficient (ih-FISH-uhnt) capable of producing desired results without wasting materials, time, or energy

fueled (FYOOD) powered

highways (HYE-wayz) main roads that connect cities and towns

maintenance (MAYN-tuh-nuhns) the act of keeping equipment in good condition by making repairs

manufacturers (man-yuh-FAK-chur-urz) companies that make a product

performance (pur-FOR-muhns) how well someone or something works

production (pruh-DUHK-shuhn) the process of making something for sale or use

upgrade (UHP-grade) something that is better because it includes the most recent improvements

FIND OUT MORE

BOOKS

Gitlin, Martin. *Careers in Self-Driving Car Technology*. Ann Arbor, MI: Cherry Lake Publishing, 2018.

Zuchora-Walske, Christine. *Self-Driving Cars*. Minneapolis, MN: Checkerboard Library, 2017.

WEBSITES

DK Find Out!—History of Cars
https://www.dkfindout.com/us/transportation/history-cars
Learn about the different types of cars over the past century.

Kiddle—Henry Ford Facts for Kids
https://kids.kiddle.co/Henry_Ford
Learn more about Henry Ford and his invention.

INDEX

air pollution, 19
assembly line, 6, 7

Beetle, 12, 13

cars
    boom after World
        War II, 10–15
    driverless, 20–21
    early, 7–9
    electric, 18–21
    improvements, 9, 13
    most popular, 13
    self-driving, 19, 21
Cord Automobile, 8

driverless cars, 20

Eisenhower, Dwight D.,
    14
electric cars, 18–21

factories, 11
Ford, Henry, 5, 6

gas, 16, 17
Germany, 13

highways, 15

Model T, 4–6, 7

oil, 17

"People's Car," 12
pollution, 19

roads, 14, 15, 21

self-driving cars, 19, 21

Tin Lizzie, 4–6

Volkswagen, 12, 13

World War II, 11

ABOUT THE AUTHOR

Jennifer Colby is a school librarian in Ann Arbor, Michigan. She loves reading, traveling, and going to museums to learn about new things.